PASSIVE INCOME ONLINE

5 Highly Profitable Ways To Make Money Online

JONATHAN S. WALKER

Copyright © 2017 Jonathan S. Walker
All rights reserved.

DEDICATION

This Book Is Dedicated To All Who Desire To Be Financially Free. May Your Efforts Bear Fruits In the Near Future And I Wish You All The Success In Life.

&

I dedicate this book as well to my two beautiful children and my loving wife who have been nothing short of being my light and joy throughout the years.

CONTENTS

	Introduction	1
1	Chapter 1: Create An Ebook Empire	6
2	Chapter 2: Create Killer Blogs	12
3	Chapter 3: Creating Your Own Youtube Channel	23
4	Chapter 4: Sell With Amazon FBA	29
5	Chapter 5: Create Membership Sites	36
6	Conclusion	43

⚓ Copyright 2017 by Jonathan S. Walker - All rights reserved.

The following eBook is reproduced below with the goal of providing information that is as accurate and reliable as possible. Regardless, purchasing this eBook can be seen as consent to the fact that both the publisher and the author of this book are in no way experts on the topics discussed within and that any recommendations or suggestions that are made herein are for entertainment purposes only. Professionals should be consulted as needed prior to undertaking any of the action endorsed herein.

This declaration is deemed fair and valid by both the American Bar Association and the Committee of Publishers Association and is legally binding throughout the United States.

Furthermore, the transmission, duplication or reproduction of any of the following work including specific information will be considered an illegal act irrespective of if it is done electronically or in print. This extends to creating a secondary or tertiary copy of the work or a recorded copy and is only allowed with express written consent from the Publisher. All additional right reserved.

The information in the following pages is broadly considered to be a truthful and accurate account of facts and as such any inattention, use or misuse of the information in question by the reader will render any resulting actions solely under their purview. There are no scenarios in which the publisher or the original author of this work can be in any fashion deemed liable for any hardship or damages that may befall them after undertaking information described herein.

Additionally, the information in the following pages is intended only for informational purposes and should thus be thought of as universal. As befitting its nature, it is presented without assurance regarding its prolonged validity or interim quality. Trademarks that are men

INTRODUCTION

Haven't you heard every successful internet entrepreneur worth his courses and blogs talk obsessively about passive income? Their focus is always on creating solid, multiple and life-long streams of wealth. So, what exactly is passive income? Why is it such a buzzword among online marketers? Why is everyone scurrying to harness the power of the internet to create income streams that last forever?

We've all been a part of the daily grind that trades time for money. We trade specific numbers of hours and get paid for only those many hours. And there's a perpetual financial crunch when it comes to meeting our expenses. To fill the gap, we take on part-time jobs, work overtime, work weekends and unfortunately, it is still not enough. We are still trading time for money. There are but 24 hours in a day, and there's only so much we can make if our income is equivalent to the time and effort we put in a day. How then does one experience exponential growth in income without spending a fortune? How does one always have enough money to enjoy the good things life without slogging night and day? Passive income is the key.

Notice how some people have all the time in the world but no money to enjoy the time at hand, while others have all the money they need but no time to enjoy the money since they are busy using that time to make money. Passive income gives you both. The time to enjoy the money you earn and the money to enjoy the time at hand. Unfortunately, a majority of the folks are so caught up in the concept of financial security that they sacrifice their financial freedom for it. True financial freedom comes when you have both time and money to enjoy your life without thinking about where the money for your next bill will come from.

As life progresses, you realize that you've traded financial freedom for financial security, where your time, income and efforts are controlled by someone else. You realize that you've been a bucket carrier all your life who goes to work on a particular day, works according to the dictates of others and then brings home a bucket of water (income). Contrast this with passive income, which is more like building a pipeline of wealth. When you create a pipeline of capital, the water automatically flows from the tap whenever you want it to. You don't have to go out and put in hours of hard work and time to get the water home in a bucket. When you create powerful, practical and multiple sources of income – the income simply comes gushing to your house. It isn't a natural process of course, but nothing in life that's worth having is ever easy. It may take days or months to create a pipeline, but it is a one-time effort that can give you a lifelong source of income. To quote an oft repeated internet marketing cliché which is indeed true, with the passive income you literally make money while you are sleeping. Or holidaying in the Alps. Or attending your child's school function. You do not have to work large numbers of hours to rake in a substantial income.

Now there are many ways to earn passive income. You may think of owning real estate and leasing it out as a form of passive income. Then some investments can give you a sound passive income based on the interests these investments generate. However, think about the upfront investments these sources of income require. Purchasing pricey real estate or setting aside a huge sum for investment purposes is no mean feat. You may make a decent amount of passive income in return, but the investment may just not make it worth it.

Let us look at online passive income streams now.

They require minimal investment and can help you witness exponential financial growth. Other than a low investment, all you need is time and information to get started, and you may well be on your way to creating a treasure house of income. Most well-known online entrepreneurs didn't start as millionaires. They barely had enough money to pay their bills and sustain. They were just perceptive, tenacious and resourceful enough to channelize the power of the internet to create smart income streams. There's no reason why you cannot do the same.

This book has just about everything you need to know about building passive income streams online. I have tried my best to share the little-known strategies and proven secret sauce that differentiates average internet marketers from the really successful ones. There are lots of actionable points and nuggets of wisdom that can help you build strong, diverse sources of passive income online with little investment. You will learn how to think out of the box and become an innovative online entrepreneur. More than anything - you will discover the joy and gratification of creating sources of wealth that give you greater freedom. Think -the freedom to spend time with your loved ones, the freedom to live life on your terms and the freedom to work for your profits rather than the net profits of a corporation. Get on the passive income lane now and enjoy the ride!

Chapter 1: Create an eBook Empire

Well yes, the truth is – people are loving eBooks. A comprehensive 2012 survey by Pew Research Center discovered that about 43 percent of Americans read a book or long content (journals, magazines, etc.) on an electronic device. The survey also revealed about 28 percent Americans owned a minimum of one electronic reading device. You can only imagine how much the numbers would have grown since. Packed with practicality (well, even the biggest home library may not be able to accommodate a million books), portability and quick access, eBooks are transforming the way people read. Why not cash in on this wonderful development and create some useful, information-packed and exciting books that will add value to people's lives? Here's all the meat and juice for creating your own successful eBook empire.

Find a Passion

We all have that one thing which lights the fire in us. What is that one topic or niche which you can talk on or write about for hours? Fitness? Psychic powers? Cooking? Raising children? Write down a list of possible ideas you can think of which you see yourself writing with knowledge and passion. Build mind maps once you've decided on the core topic. These can include all the sub-topics you may want to include within the main subject. For instance, if you are putting together a fitness related eBook, think of all the chapters/sub-topics/sub niches to be included in it.

This can be fitness workouts, diets to complement your workouts, ideal fitness attire, fitness gear, fitness stretches and the likes. Similarly, if you find the marketplace is already crowded with too many fitness related books, you can narrow down your focus to a single aspect of fitness. Say Post Pregnancy Fitness – How to Get Back in Shape After Having a Baby. If you are already an expert in a particular niche, such as a child psychologist or real estate attorney or wedding planner, jump right in within your area of expertise.

Start Writing

Once you have a topic in place, begin a rough table of contents draft for the book. This will help you flesh out the topics later. You can use any word processor such as Notepad or Word. Some people prefer Evernote. If you are not comfortable writing it as a single document, break down the documents chapter-wise. This way you can move around and access various chapters quickly and then put them together in the end.

You will have to play around with images, font sizes, colors and headers to make huge chunks of text easy to read. Make the book look attractive, easy on the eye and navigation friendly. In the end, put all the chapters together to create a seamless flow.

Convert It into an eBook

A simple Google search should give you multiple options for converting a word document into an eBook. You simply need to upload a Word file, and it is transformed into an eBook. A calibre is a free software that can be downloaded and used for word processor to eBook conversion. Go through everything to ensure the formatting is in place. There's a preview tool that lets you see a final version of the book, so you know exactly how the formatting will appear on electronic devices.

Create A Stunning Cover

You can create a gorgeous looking eBook cover using either some type of graphic software program such as Photoshop or Ms. Office (Powerpoint, Word, etc.). You can also hire the services of expert graphic designers on freelance project sites. Look at other covers for inspiration. Once you have a design and layout in mind, create and upload it. Amazon also has a handy cover creator, which can be used for building quick and effective eBook covers. Amazon will only display your book cover in the "Customers Who Bought This Item Also Bought" to trigger reader curiosity. Ensure that it is sharp, attention-grabbing and relevant.

Pricing Your eBook

Amazon gives you the option of picking your own book pricing plan. You can either avail 35 percent profits by setting your own price or 70 percent profits by pricing your book according to Amazon's prescribed price between $2.99 to $9.99. Unless there is a strong business plan behind pricing your book outside $2.99 to$ 9.99, it makes sense to keep a significant chunk of your profits.

Promote The Book Extensively

Amazon will only boost your sale and reach when you fulfill the requirement of their sophisticated algorithms. You will have to promote and push your book initially to get support from them. This can be done by creating a few high-quality guest blog posts on sites/blogs related to your book. You can include a snippet about the book in the author bio to pique the interest of readers. Another great way is to take interesting and meaningful lines from your book and convert them into quote memes or tweets. Lots of people sharing and re-tweeting them will help you garner a large audience. Include a link to your book wherever permissible. Social media updates, blogs, email signatures and the likes.

A good way to build a bank of reviews and customers is to distribute free copies to people within your social network and ask them for genuine reviews. You can also price the book at a discounted rate in the early launch stages and ask the first few buyers to write reviews, before changing to the regular price. It always helps to have some reviews in there when readers are trying to make purchase related choices.

Another advantage of having a lot of early buyers is that Amazon boosts popular titles and gives it, even more, exposure once they see a lot of people picking it up. This can massively help your rankings.

Other Publishing Channels

Other than Kindle Publishing, you can also publish your book on your own website. It may not enjoy a roaring exposure initially or at least not as much as a large platform like Amazon, however over a period of time; you can enjoy higher profits. Third party hosting merchants may charge you a small percentage fee of about 1 to 5 percent for accepting customer payments and delivering the content to them in a downloadable format.

Chapter 2: Creating Killer Blogs

Blog- the internet marketer's golden word. And rightly so. Imagine creating a single valuable, detailed, comprehensive and well-researched post just once and earning from it years after you have published it. Blogs can be used in tandem with other passive income sources such as membership-based training programs or eBooks. They can also be stand-alone income generators. You can earn revenue through advertising programs such as Google Adsense. Then there's the highly lucrative world of affiliate marketing and list building. Selling banner advertisements, physical products, courses, eBooks and more is just the tip of the iceberg. There is really so much you can do with an informative, valuable and content-packed blog.

Pack Value Which is Tough To Find Elsewhere

Pick a topic you are passionate about and know well.

Do not incredible trend hop and know what topics are popular. Yes, you need to do basic keyword research to determine if there's sufficient demand for your niche but don't obsess too much about finding the most populated niches. The challenge is to grab any niche you like and make it popular! Go with specific topics or sub niches to laser target your audience and gain monopoly within the sub-niche. For instance, if you find that weight loss is an overcrowded niche, try dominating a sub-niche such as a post pregnancy weight loss or weight loss for seniors. This way you get a more focused audience who you can sell and market to with comparatively lesser competition.

Create Interesting and Valuable Content

Create original, engaging, unique and useful content that gives your readers more value. Explore your expertise and write about something that you have a sound knowledge or background of. Use powerful elements to support your text such as images, videos, and infographics. Use screenshots wherever required to make the content clearer for your target audience. This will require more time and effort than a simple text blog. However, it will help your search engine rankings and will give you lots of loyal readers.

Choose A Blogging Platform

If you are serious about starting a blog that generates passive income, avoid using a free blogging platform and opt for the WordPress self-hosted medium. WordPress is one of the most widely used, customizable, easy to operate and visually stunning blogging platforms. The self-hosted option allows you to set up banner advertisements and use affiliate market links within the blog. Your blog URL looks more professional, in addition to the fact that you will be able to play with abundant features for beautifying your blog. Find a reliable hosting service and a brandable, memorable and unique domain name.

Blog Interface

If content is the king, your blog design is the queen. It will determine many factors such as the stickiness of your blog, the time people spend on your blog, the click through rate of your links and much more. Opt for a clean, well-defined and user-friendly interface. Use can either use a WordPress theme or buy them from a third party like Themeforest.net. You can also pick between free and paid themes. Paid themes add more bells and whistles to your blog to make it look attention grabbing and professional. Themes can be changed instantly by going to the Appearances section of your WordPress admin panel. Ensure you pick a responsive theme for your blog as a majority of users access the Internet from handheld devices. Make it easy for visitors to find everything on your blog by organizing all relevant tabs on your home page. Balance colors well, and leave enough white space to give the eye some relief. Use customized headers created by a professional graphic artist. Improve the readability of your blog by using subheads, bullets, text bubbles for critical text, tables, charts, illustrations and more. This helps attention starved people pick key points from your content without having to go through the entire piece.

Monetizing The Blog

Advertising Program – You can 'rent' out space on your site to popular advertising programs such as Google Adsense, Yahoo Bing Network, Clicksor and more. These ad networks keep the advertisements relevant to your blog content and pay you a small amount every time a visitor on your site clicks on the advertisement. The best part is you aren't creating or selling any products but merely using the space on your blog to create passive income.

Affiliate Marketing – Affiliate marketing is all about selling other people's products on your site and earning a commission on every sale or lead that is fulfilled through a link on your blog. Say for instance, you run a pet travel site and have a steady stream of pet owners who travel with their pets. You can sign up as an affiliate for a puppy discipline informational eBook or a nationwide network of pet care and grooming services. So each time a pet owner buys the book or signs up for the pet grooming services, you get a nice little commission. Though individual products and services may have their own affiliate program, some popular marketplaces where you can find several affiliate programs are Clickbank, Offervault, Markethealth, ShareASale, Commission Junction and Avangate.

1. Review Writing – Writing useful, comprehensive and well-researched reviews is one of the best ways to sink your teeth into the world of affiliate

marketing. Identify high-quality products with top-notch customer support, which can be really useful for your audience. Draft lengthy reviews to promote the products (include both pros and cons) and make your buyer's decision making process simpler. Reviews are often sought by people who are already half way within the buying cycle (with some options at hand) and giving them a good overview of the product will help you complete the sale.

2. Promote The Right Products - This should be fairly obvious yet it is surprising how many folks get it all wrong when it comes to promoting the right products. Find products that feature high ratings, superior quality, decent recommendations and most important - are relevant for your audience. Promoting dubious products and scams spell doom for affiliate marketers. You might make those first few sales by luring people, however your long term credibility may take a massive blow. If you plan to

stick around for long and build a dependable source of passive income, pick your products judiciously.

3. Think Out Of The Box – If you believe the virtual world is already choc-a-bloc with multiple affiliate offers, think out of the box and act as an affiliate for local businesses. Use conventional businesses to generate profitable commissions. For example, let us assume you run an interior design and decorator blog that gives people interesting home makeover ideas. You can tie up with home improvement companies, contractors and furniture suppliers in your neighborhood for lead capturing or selling their products to your readers. You may also be running a city or region based blog, and promoting local businesses may be the perfect passive income business model.

4. Diversity – Diversify your affiliate marketing offers, yet do not crowd your blog with too many sales pitches. Pick a handful of good offers and start

promoting them. For example, for a travel blog, you can promote multiple products/programs such as backpacks, a traveler blogger training program, photography equipment and more. This way you are catering to diverse needs and pulling in bigger profits.

5. Links – Use link cloakers to get rid of the ugly, long and unprofessional looking affiliate links. They make your links appear cleaner, shorter and more professional, while also boosting your click-through figures. Another pro tip is to make the visuals on your blog clickable. When images are made clickable by linking back to the sales page of the offer you are promoting, enthusiastic customers are immediately led to the relevant buying page. When you are eagerly looking to buy something or thinking about buying something, you don't want a tacky looking image upload page to play mood killer. User experience is a huge factor in determining the

success of your affiliate marketing blog.

6. Selling Banner Ads – Once your blog attains considerable popularity, you can consider selling banner ad spaces to businesses related to your blog. You have complete control over how much you charge these firms since you are directly dealing with them. If you draw impressive traffic figures from a well-targeted audience, companies will be willing to negotiate lucrative advertising revenue.

7. Selling Informational Products – Selling your own digital products is another source of passive income. These can eBooks, short reports, email courses or membership programs. If you have high-quality, original and problem-solving content on your blogs, you will build a loyal base of readers who trust your expertise. They will be more than happy to buy informational products from you. The book can be sold to your mail subscribers or directly on your blog/website using an attention-grabbing landing

page.

8. Directory Listings – When your blog becomes somewhat popular, you can start a paid listings section and rake in a good amount of income from it. The services can be related to your blog content. For instance, if you are running a blog related to wedding planning, and pull in a massive traffic of soon to be brides, you can put up listings of professionals offering wedding related services such as florists, bakers, decorators, jewelers and travel companies. This helps to add an extra income avenue to your blog. Passive income is all about diversifying and optimizing revenue from a single source.

9. Pay Per Lead For Local Businesses – Imagine you have a thriving blog that focuses on real estate and attracts lots of real estate buyers and sellers who are hungry for information. How about working out an arrangement with local real estate

firms/professionals to pay you per buyer/seller lead you send them? Leads can be captured by informing your audience that you can help them find some of the best properties in their area. It is a win-win situation for all. Again, passive income is thinking out of the box and leveraging multiple income streams to maximize your profits.

10. Promotions and Paid Recommendations/Reviews – Once you gain considerable authority in your niche and are often referred to as an industry influencer, you can easily do paid reviews/recommendations or draft promotional posts. At this stage, you will most likely have a large following of people who trust your opinion. Cash in on it by promoting others' products and services through promotional posts. Make sure that you don't fill your blog solely with promotional posts and maintain a delicate balance between promotional and non-promotional content. The idea is not merely to sell to your target

audience, but to help them buy by recommending really great stuff which makes their life simpler.

11. List Building – A blog that attracts a steady stream of targeted visitors can be great for list building. Place a sign-up box prominently on your blog to attract a swarm of organic subscribers from well-targeted traffic. These are a bunch of already interested action takers, and you could sell just about any related offers, programs, courses, services and products to them. When people sign up for a mailing list, they are voluntarily expressing their interest in knowing more about the products/services being promoted by you. These leads can be used to generate a decent amount of passive income by boosting your sales conversions.

To get potential customers to sign up for your list, make them an offer they can't refuse. Throw in a free eBook or offer them a 10-15 day course. You can also include your affiliate links within the eBook or course. For example, if you are offering an eBook that offers WordPress site creation to beginners, you may want to suggest a good domain name registration and hosting service. Sign up as an affiliate of a reputed web hosting and domain name service and recommend it to your buyers in the course of the book.

Chapter 3: Create Your Own YouTube Channel

Did you know that YouTube has 60 hours of video uploaded to it every 60 seconds? Or that more than 4 billion videos are watched every day? The platform gets a crazy 800 million unique visitors every month (source – Jeffbullas.com). There is a marked shift from consuming text related content to content that is more interactive and real time. Users with small attention spans find it way more convenient to see something than reading about it. Also, the demand for video-based content is at an all-time high, with lesser competition than text-based blogs. Not many people are confident about facing the camera, and that's where you can cash in while space is relatively less crowded.

Belonging To The Big G Family Helps

Since YouTube comes from the Google stable, it is hugely favored by the big G in their organic search results. If you optimize your video for search engines by using the right keywords in the title, meta tags, and descriptions, your videos will enjoy higher placement rankings in search results. It is much easier to get a YouTube video to rank on Google compared to a blog post.

Go With Technical and Problem Solving Topics

The nature of YouTube fits very well with technical and problem-solving topics where people are looking for very specific solutions. For instance, someone may want to know how to create a table of contents in MS Word or the basics of using MS Excel. Isn't it easier to get a step by step demonstration of using these features rather than only reading about them? Similarly, cooking, DIY crafts, and product demonstrations are extremely popular on YouTube. When users watch videos on your YouTube channel, there are related ads that pop up on the screen. When visitors click on these ads, you get paid for it. This is why it is emphasized that you have a focused and clear problem-solving niche. Comedians or other

YouTube performers may not enjoy much ad relevancy since they do not have a very targeted audience. However, if you are extremely popular, you may make a considerable income even with low click through rates.

Unconventional ways to approach a common topic works wonderfully on YouTube. Throw in a lot of wit, creativity, visual play and humor to illustrate complex topics. Offer interesting metaphors and analogies, and include surprise elements that make your audience take notice.

Use Your Watermark For Videos

Always use a watermark of your blog for your videos. This way users will know exactly where the videos originated from, which will make it easier for them to track your blog and channel. Some users may embed your video on their site. Having a clear watermark with your blog's name can drive more traffic and create a brand identity. Since descriptions only show up on YouTube and not other blogs where your video might be embedded, your URL can be made visible in the watermark.

Start With An Overview

Though videos are easier to watch than elaborate pieces of text, getting a user to watch an entire video is going be a challenge. How do you ensure that users are glued to your videos until the end? Simple. Just begin with an interesting overview of everything that's included in the video. This whets their appetite and keeps them hooked. This breaks the ice with your user, engages them and boosts their chances of sticking around. Get them interested and enthusiastic about what you are covering in your video. Make an interesting visual summary or map about what's coming up next. Giving them pointers about upcoming content is an excellent way to make them stay.

Create A Fantastic Call To Action

All your efforts of filming spectacular videos with the best sound and visual effects can be pointless if you do not include a compelling and impactful call to action at the end of it. Including a bright and attention-grabbing call to action ensures you don't leave your viewers high and dry after getting them interested with the video. They should know exactly what to do next if they want to know more about your products or services. Ask them to visit your website or blog or follow you on various social networks. If they sit through the entire video, they most likely are in a more positive and action oriented state of mind to follow what you tell them to do.

Optimize Your Videos

One solid tip for optimizing your YouTube videos and making them more findable is to include your main keyword in the title followed by a subtitle that lists your secondary keyword and is a rephrased version of the main title. For instance, if you have a video talking about various retirement plans, you can title as Retirement Saving Plans: 30 Brilliant Tips For Planning a Hassle-Free Retirement.

Also, ensure your video descriptions are keyword optimized, appealing, clear and descriptive. This makes it easy for search engines to place them at the top of relevant searches.

Leverage The Trailer Video Feature

If you want to convert walk-in or browse through viewers into loyal subscribers, utilize You Tube's trailer video feature optimally. The platform allows you to include a video at the top of your channel to give nonsubscribers a glimpse of your channel. This acts as a teaser to pique your audience's curiosity. Make a compelling, sticky and appealing trailer video to bag more subscribers.

Another super layout tip is to opt for the Player view over Grid View. Unlike Grid View, Player view sets a single large video on auto-play.

Be Prolific And Upload Frequently

There are no two ways about it. If you are looking to generate passive income from your YouTube channel, you must keep adding content prolifically. The more videos you have out there and the more consistently you post these videos, the higher are your chances of creating a decent income bank. Create an editorial planner and plan to post your videos at regular intervals.

Create and upload videos that talk about different aspects of your niche/topic/industry to build an influential channel. For example, if you run a YouTube channel related to post-pregnancy weight loss fitness regimes, try and include other related information such as healthy recipes for new mothers or post pregnancy wardrobe ideas or newborn baby care tips. Try and explore the topic from varied angles, so visitors keep coming back for more.

Chapter 4: Sell With Amazon FBA

Dropshipping is another convenient and lucrative online passive income option. A large number of virtual entrepreneurs prefer the drop shipping business model for its flexibility and simplicity. You don't need space to maintain a product inventory. Similarly, there is a minimal capital investment in setting up an e-commerce venture. While FBA (Fulfillment By Amazon) requires a flexible product investment, regular drop shipping doesn't need any upfront product investment.

The orders are fulfilled by a retail giant such as Amazon, while you get to make a tidy profit behind every sale. The best part about this business is that you can sell a huge variety of products without having to worry about maintaining a large inventory. There's little wonder that FBA has become one of the most popular home business ventures.

FBA is a super way to leverage the power of Amazon

for making profits. You do not have to deal with the sales, buyers or shipping process. Your only job is to source products and send them to Amazon for maintaining your inventory. Your products receive massive exposure in marketplaces. They store your product within their network of warehouses and deliver it to your customers. Heck, they even offer customer service. Couldn't be simpler, could it? An excellent way to rake in passive income, you say? Well yes and no. It is convenient and simple, but not a get rich overnight scheme. You need to invest considerable time and efforts in researching and identifying products that will sell like hot cakes. You will also need to find suppliers and negotiate prices with them. However, once you are all set, it can't get any more passive than this. You literally don't have to do anything to bring in sales and deliver orders.

Upfront Costs

Unlike dropshipping, you will need a small

investment to put together a product inventory for FBA and ship it to Amazon's warehouses. Other than physical product and forwarding charges, expenses you will incur include Amazon's referral fee, subscription fees (either 0.99/transaction or $39.99 monthly plan) and inventory storing fees.

The FBA calculator helps you work a selling price by considering exact fees and shipping charges. Your aim is to find unique products that people need at the right price and price them correctly to maximize your profits. The investment is completely up to the seller. You can buy products worth $10000 or $500. Start small to test your markets and scale up once you see results. Invest as much as you can afford to lose, pick your products carefully and price them judiciously.

If you are just getting your feet wet in FBA or sell more big ticket items in small quantities, you may be better off picking the $0.99/transaction subscription fee option. This plan lets you sell up to 40 products a month. However, if you reckon selling more than 40 products each month, it makes sense to sign up for the $39.99 monthly fee. This is good value for serious folks who plan to carry out hundreds of transactions each month. There are plenty of addition features, such as generating business reports in the latter.

The FBA Edge

What are the benefits of selling on FBA?

FBA items rank higher when people search for specific products. They also show up frequently on the recommended buy box option, even over items that are priced lower. Buyers are almost always likelier to opt for recommended products.

FBA products are eligible for Amazon Prime membership benefits like complimentary next day delivery, thus making Prime members much more likely to purchase these products.

You get access to a fantastic and widely used sales platform, enjoy higher search rankings, and a well-oiled, almost automated system that helps you generate huge profits consistently.

Signing Up For FBA

You can either register for an FBA account with your existing credentials or create a brand new account. Pick your subscription plan depending on the number of products you expect to sell. You can either use your company's legal name or your name. Fill in your credit card number and other details. Credit card details are shared upfront so your account can be charged in the event that you run into a deficit. This can occur when you do not have any sales, yet have to bear warehouse storage and subscription fees.

Next, pick your display name. Remember, this is your brand identity. Make it unique, memorable and likable. Your audience must be able to identify and relate to it. It should be relevant to your niche if you are focusing on a specific group of products.

You will be required to confirm your identity with a phone call or text message. This completes your registration process. Fill in your bank account details so your earnings can be directly deposited into your account. The deposit method can be selected by going to the Setting tab and picking an option from the scroll down under Account Info. Verify your bank details to start receiving payments.

At this stage, you are an Amazon Seller but not yet registered for FBA. Now, visit the FBA registration page and hit on Getting Started to launch your FBA seller account.

Finding the Right Products

To begin with, you will have to be on the look-out for bargains and then measure them up against existing Amazon listings to anticipate how they will perform in comparison with competing products. How much can you sell the product for? Are the products likely to sell? Checking out existing products will answer these crucial questions. Use the Amazon Bestsellers list as a reference point to identify your star products. A product rank under rank 1000 in a relatively large category means it is faring reasonably well and can be considered for your inventory list.

Register to receive newsletter updates from reputed wholesalers or be a part of the mailing list of stores such Ikea and Walmart. They may send you special promos and offers or you can browse their website for popular or unique products. If you find a product that can be sourced really cheaply due to a limited period discount, try and order it in bulk and include it in your inventory. This way you can keep selling the product at a much higher price and rake in cool profits. Do not forget to take Amazon's fees into consideration while working out the price.

Private Label Products

Private label products are sold under your own brand name. You can source products in bulk directly from the manufacturer or wholesaler, and package the product with your label. You are therefore positioning the product as if it is being manufactured or supplied by your own firm.

Chapter 5: Create Membership Sites

Membership sites can help you rake in a good amount of passive income for a long time if you have a particular expertise that is sought after by plenty of people, especially knowledge related to the virtual world. You may be an expert in creating smartphone apps or copywriting or web designing or basically anything that people actively seek to learn. It can also be related to DIY and hobby based pursuits. How about language learning if you have mastery over a particular language or drone making if you know how to put together incredible drones?

At the onset, it is important to understand that membership sites need hard-work. You always have to keep updating, adding value, provide novel information and much more to keep your paid subscribers hooked. You must offer beyond exceptional value to retain your subscribers, which means it may not be a good option if you are just starting out in the online business world. Once you gain sufficient experience in a domain, you can consider launching your own membership site based business model. If you possess unique skills or knowledge which is in-demand, you can jump into it after doing some basic groundwork. Since information is widely available everywhere, you must have something really unique to offer your audience if you expect them to pay for it.

Adding Membership Option To Existing Blogs

If your blog is already popular among a group of readers/users who are demanding more in-depth information from you, create a membership site and give them what they are looking for. For instance, if you run a blog that gives people ideas about what topics they can blog about or blog niche ideas and your audience suggest that you also include comprehensive keywords/keyword research reports for different niches, you can charge a premium membership fee for the detailed information. If you already have a blog or website, you simply need to add a membership site plug-in to it.

Start With a Few Complimentary Slots

Start by giving out the first few slots for free to build some response and reviews for your membership based site. The most positive and active folks on your mailing list, who are always adding value in the form of suggestions or discussions, can be considered for the giveaway. You can also consider giving away the first few slots at a discounted price with a coupon mailed to your loyal subscribers.

You may have a set of people who are regularly commenting on your blog posts or social media, while also contributing meaningfully to the discussions and helping other members. Make them your evangelists. Make them feel privileged by offering them free membership, and let them spread the word about your membership site.

Focus on Creating A Loyal Community

Membership sites are as much about a supportive and loyal community feel as they are about power packed information. The information will pretty much fade away over a period of time. However, the relationship you build with your customers and the loyalty you inspire in them by adding value to their lives is what will keep them from leaving. Membership sites are all about creating a dedicated community of users where people support each other, resolve each other's queries and offer valuable guidance. Build a passionate following on the social media, and create a learning forum where members can swap ideas and solve other's issues. Ensure that you are prompt in your response when subscribers mail you with an issue.

Always ask for feedback from active subscribers. What aspects of the topic do they want to know more about? What other tools and software they need to optimize their results? What are the most common issues they come across while doing what you teach them to? Opinion polls are a good way of identify the general sentiment related to various topics. You can build on topics that have been well-accepted and drop the ones that do not add much value.

You need to know exactly what your customers are looking for to hand it to them on a platter. Unscreen is a handy tool for monitoring and analyzing your audience activity. It lets you know which content type is generating optimal traction so you can create more of those.

Create High-Quality build

Tutorials and guides are much sought after in today's information-packed digital world. People are looking for easier ways to perform multiple tasks. And what better to train people than to create high quality, interactive and information rich real time or pre-recorded videos. One of the biggest advantages of these videos is that they can be accessed by followers across the world according to their convenience. Ask questions, conduct polls and stimulate discussions to inspire greater user interactivity. This will keep your audience glued from start to finish.

Use high quality and evocative visuals to make the matter more interesting and digestible. Visuals can be creatively weaved into the narrative to explain tricky concepts. You need to have a rough draft of how your presentation will flow, even if you aim to keep it more spontaneous. Create a rough table of topics, which you can elaborate on during the course of the webinar. If you are catering to a more global audience, use more universally accepted words, gestures, and ideas.

Organize Your Information Efficiently

Once your site grows, you need to organize it effectively to foster better navigation and access to information for new members. Guide your members through the maze of information by putting it all together in an orderly manner. If you find that new or existing users are asking you the same questions over and over on the social media or email, you can put together a handy Q & A page for newbies. Alternatively, have an introduction or 'begin here' page in place, where you can make new members feel less overwhelmed by all the information and guide them about navigating the available information in a step-by-step manner. Keep updating this section regularly.

Include a 'blast from the past' or 'refresher' section where you can re-post popular older blogs that members might have missed or link to those posts that are currently relevant.

Record A Friendly Welcome Video

One of the best ways to establish a warm rapport with your customers, and inspire their trust and loyalty is to record a cheery greeting video. It can be anything from a demonstration of how the site works or a story or a gentle reminder of the do's and don'ts. You can tell them how they can make optimal utilization of your services or how they can contact you should they stumble upon some issues or inspiring experiences of existing members.

Bring In The Influencers

You can offer free subscriptions to authoritative figures in your industry and ask them to leave behind genuine reviews about the site. People are likelier to take their unbiased report seriously, and give your site a look through. Since influencers have a relatively large follower base, your site will enjoy a wide reach among potential subscribers.

Create Group Events

Group events and challenges are a great way to

engage existing members and keep them hooked. Motivate them and help them stay on track. It can be anything small like a challenge that helps subscribers attain a specific goal. For instance, if you run a membership site for writers who aspire to fulfill their writing goals, create a challenge video that encourages subscribers to complete a goal for the week. The buzz of working as a group/community can be wonderfully motivating and creates a strong, positive vibe. You can also have other events, team challenges (where members compete with each other), courses and similar activities frequently to keep your subscribers on their toes.

Conclusion

All you need to do now is to simply take action. Now that you are armed with the ammo of information, you can use all the practical tips and step by step plans described in the book to create your own rewarding and profitable sources of incomes. Think outside the box and build on these ideas. Be resourceful and exploit multiple income channels to create a genuinely prosperous future.

Over to you!

THANK YOU

Dear treasured reader, I would like to thank you from the bottom of my heart purchasing this valuable resource on building a passive income online. I sincerely hope the book is able to help you realize your dream of being financially free by giving you several choices and strategies for building profitable online ventures.

I hope you've gotten some valuable information that you can use daily to better your life and those around you as well. If you liked it would you be so kind as to leave an honest/positive review for my book. I would appreciate it very much.

Here's to your financially free, rewarding and profitable life.

**To Your Success,
Jonathan S. Walker**

www.ingramcontent.com/pod-product-compliance
Lightning Source LLC
LaVergne TN
LVHW010434070526
838199LV00066B/6022